Gerry &
Barbara —

Warm
Wishes!

Warren
Goldenberg

The Mysemite
Sketches

Warren Cederborg

Bloomington, IN Milton Keynes, UK

authorHOUSE®

AuthorHouse™
1663 Liberty Drive, Suite 200
Bloomington, IN 47403
www.authorhouse.com
Phone: 1-800-839-8640

AuthorHouse™ UK Ltd.
500 Avebury Boulevard
Central Milton Keynes, MK9 2BE
www.authorhouse.co.uk
Phone: 08001974150

Cover photography by author.

First published by AuthorHouse 2/27/2007

ISBN: 978-1-4259-5495-6 (sc)

Library of Congress Control Number: 2006907285

Printed in the United States of America
Bloomington, Indiana.

This book is printed on acid-free paper.

To my wife Suzie,
my brother Steve and
his wife Linda —
more a sister than a sister-in-law.

In memory of Steve Medley

Scribing the Light

Some years back, a guest at the Yosemite Lodge told me he had ushered his family into the park by announcing, "We're in Yosemite." Thinking he meant, "*Your*-semite," his young daughter replied, "We're in My-semite?"

As John Muir might have said, "Isn't it glorious that it's Her-semite, My-semite and Your-semite as well."

The Mysemite Sketches are derived from my observations in a 58-year association with the park; the sketch being a method of transforming my trail notes and journal entries into metrical form.

The *Lymanlight* grouping became an integral part of this collection when I was cabin-bound in Visalia during the winter of 1995-96. With the release of Stephen Lyman's selected work *Into the Wilderness: An Artist's Journey*, I was able to mingle my own experiences in the park with his specific paintings — my point of view from his point of view, so to speak. As light has been a key theme in my writing, I was struck by the reverence Lyman had for it.

When I came upon Lyman's wonderful work, I grew to realize that a higher authority had passed on the ability to capture the soul of Yosemite after Ansel Adams died in 1984. Although a highly accomplished photographer in his own right, Lyman was predictably humbled by the comparison. When I sent the *Lymanlight Sketches* to him in January of 1996, he wrote back saying, "Yosemite certainly continues to inspire many people."

Since his death in a climbing accident in Yosemite three months later, I have grown to realize how important Lyman's work has been in focusing my passion for the "crown jewel" of our national parks, as well as helping me to better understand her.

I have included *John's Song* in this collection for several reasons. Written in the mid-1970s and later incorporated into my unpublished manuscript *The Firefall Trilogy*, the poem is longer than a sketch but speaks volumes as to my fascination with the inherent mysteries of Yosemite. It reminds me of how I have long viewed the park as a presence — embracing, though at times frightening, and very much worthy of our respect. Also longer than the norm is *Yesterdaze*, some free-falling recollections from my childhood.

I have elected to use some of the Ahwahneechee words in my verse in the hope that they never grow antiquated. Words like *Tissiack* (Half Dome) and *Pohono* (referring to the wind in some instances and Bridalveil Fall in others) are as much a part of the park as the intriguing people who first inhabited her.

Of particular significance to me is the brief synopsis *Yosemite Chapel*, for in 1971 my wife Suzie and I were married in that rustic structure. As my best friend, Suzie has shared in many of the experiences that led to these sketches, with her support and encouragement facilitating much of my work. I find myself having to admit that I couldn't have published anything without her.

Words cannot express my gratitude to Dr. Donald Markos for his editorial assistance with this and other projects. I also wish to thank my readers Shirley Nedham and Linda Cederborg for their continuous support; and I was honored to have Jim Snyder write the introduction to this collection. His love for Yosemite and knowledge of its history might only be exceeded by his dedication to the park's preservation.

Underlying this body of verse is that the reader might gain a deepening awareness that concentration on the preservation of Yosemite must be a high priority.

In that light, I would like to recognize the Yosemite Association and the Yosemite Fund along with their generous members for joining hands with the National Park Service in heightening the quality of the visitor's experience.

Yosemite: breathe her in, take her with you, but leave her unsullied that all might see.

I must add that the joy in releasing this collection was greatly diminished when Yosemite Association President Steve Medley was killed in an automobile accident during the final stages of editing. Steve was a wealth of encouragement for all Yosemite authors and truly one of the park's best friends.

The Yosemite Mystique

Many of Warren Cederborg's readers will recognize his story of the little girl and her "Mysemite" question as one they've heard, usually from parents who particularly love retelling it. The story shows us what can happen to an outwardly odd sounding name in a child's hands, but also suggests how a special place might be altered in our perception of it. Sometimes a child's memory remains an important part of the later adult view; yet, most of the time, perceptions change as we ourselves age and change. It's up to us to recognize the changes and try to understand what they mean for us. In this book of poetic sketches Warren has tried to do that.

His parents brought Warren to Housekeeping Camp in Yosemite Valley during summers beginning in 1948. He literally grew up with Yosemite. In the '60s, he worked for Curry Company with summer beach parties and Firefalls occupying his off-duty hours. A military tour in Vietnam interrupted his Yosemite years, but also brought him quickly back. He and his wife Suzie were married in the Yosemite Chapel in 1971. First the war and then a working family life kept him from returning as often as he and his family would have liked, but those experiences and time also affected his slowly evolving perception of the place.

Warren's preferred medium for understanding Yosemite has been writing. In the poem *Little Yosemite Afternoon*, he gives us a glimpse of himself scribbling observations in the hollow of a sugar pine during a rainstorm. At first, he thought he should use this writing to see what Ansel Adams saw. Then he became acquainted with Steve Lyman's work. Steve painted what he wanted to see in animals, places, and light. He loved to play with landscapes to envision what was in them in different ways, and to see how observant his viewers were. When a rendering of his painting *Yosemite Alpenglow* first came to the park, people thought it was a photograph before realizing Steve had subtly rearranged some geography while eliminating all signs of human structures in Yosemite Valley. With a few brush strokes he'd implemented his version of the 1980 General Management Plan. Lyman worked hard to gain a firsthand view of what he painted in all seasons and every kind of weather in order to experience the scene he was thinking about painting. After going off into the snow to figure out what he wanted to paint in *Warmed by the View*, he returned to check in with an impish grin and twinkle in his eye: "You weren't worried about me, were you?" Unfortunately, one day he pushed too far, got stuck in Cathedral Rocks during a storm while looking for views of the Three Brothers and Horsetail Fall for new paintings, and died of a hypothermia-induced fall.

Steve's approach to art affected Warren's own as he realized he could use his own eyes and didn't have to be like Ansel Adams. Through his paintings, Steve taught Warren to "lighten up," so to speak, and see his own Yosemite, "Mysemite," in new ways. In the poem *On Stephen Lyman's Birthday*, Warren stood atop Eagle Peak as the realization sunk in:

recalling the windows he opened

to a place I thought I knew,

sampling his understanding,

and warmed by the view.

Many of Warren's sketches encapsulate those slow revelations about a place and about himself. He recalls his early camping in the Valley. He is clearly nostalgic for some earlier Yosemite traditions like the Firefall, discontinued in 1968, or Camp 7, closed after the 1997 flood. Yet he is willing to let them go, partly because what he sees from the trails or the top of Half Dome has not changed as much as his perspective of it. In his sketches of the Valley, camping and trails, Wawona and Steve Lyman's paintings, Warren Cederborg encourages you to do the same thing with your Yosemite: work hard for beauty, make it new, and make it part of you.

Jim Snyder

Retired National

Park Service Historian,

Yosemite

Tough
measuring up
to Muir;
even tougher
shuffling along
a paper trail,
searching
for identity.

Yosemitelight

Road to Glory

Downsizing
　　the highways,
I feel
　　Yosemite
　　　taking hold,
from foothills
　　to mountains
　　　with their alpine glow,
　　rising up
　　　on waves of evergreen
　　　　to Sierra soul —
that safety zone
　　from dial tones
　　　and growing old.

Yosemitelight

How in the close
　　of each bless-ed day,
I find myself
　　— squinting —
　　　to catch your last ray,
　　before shutting my eyes
　　　to let you burn
　　　　on the inside.

Beginning at the Start

So much to see
    in a Valley
        crammed with humanity.

Where does one start?

Start within yourself,
    a few paces from your stay.

Wait 'til others scurry off
— hell bent
    on a see-it-all day.

Then when
    you find yourself alone
    — so far from
        the bumper-
            to-bumper grind —
    look around and relish
    what's left behind.

Blundering Along

Following the trail
as best I can,
trying not to tromp
on all
there is
to see
— riches —
one misstep
from obscurity.

In Spite of Myself

Get up to speed WC,
      there's a huge world out there
— a cybersphere
    of jet lag,
      Taj Mahals
        and Great Walls.

There's so much to see!

A globe that's on the go
    in jumbo jets and ATV's,
      while you're stuck in Yosemite.

Folks are sipping Coladas
    and catching waves,
  while you're busting your butt
    on the John Muir Trail.

The good life's at your command
  — my friend —
    so what is it
      you don't understand?

Oversight

Mock orange and azaleas
　　along the walk,
　　　　on a village loop
　　　　　　over Sentinel Bridge and back,
　　hidden before by indifference.

Far from the Swarm

Slip away
    from the horde
to the quiet
    on the Valley floor;
follow the lupine
    from Bridalveil
    to Curry;
shadow the north wall
    from Mirror Meadow
    to El Capitan;
loop the Lodge
    and Tenaya Canyon
— get acquainted
    with the place;
or simply sit
    beside the river,
and let the breeze
    inspect your face.

Case for Escape

Today a refuge
    from San Joaquin heat;
last week, one last peek
    at dogwood in bloom;
other times,
    roaring cascades or fall shades;
whatever it takes
    to break away.

Trail's End

Muir said
    coming here
      is coming home
— a place
    to bare
    every care
and let
    your soul take hold.

The Other Valley

Hetch Hetchy,
    O'Shaughnessy
        or whatever you call
           the Tuolumne.

Blast away
    at the concrete
        of yesterday —
    let God's handiwork
        be enshrined.

Make cityites
    — guzzle —
        an alternate site.

Let the door
    of Muir's temple
        swing wide.

Drink not
from the acres
of litter,
but from the wine
of a Tuolumne design.

Impressions in Stone

From hammerstone
    to bedrock,
the hands of the ages
    pound acorn
      and consecrate the land,
both Miwok and Paiute
— the daughters of Ahwahnee —
    prepare
      what the oak provides,
while returning
    what's left
      to the ground.

To Julia Parker for keeping the
the Native American ways alive.

Twilight Fire

Rise
   highborn pines
  to timeworn skies,
   while toasty flames
    — warm —
 all that remains
   of a wondering fool
    and yesterday's Muir.

Sweet Solitude

Wandering away
  from a gadabout day,
  you step off the path
    to a place by the stream,
  some space of your own,
    to listen and feel
  attune with the breeze
    — at home —
      in Ahwahnee.

Passing Cathedral

Bend by bend
    the river runs
  — patiently —
brimming with life
    toward a managed end,
   to be guttered
    out to sea,
then rise again,
  to fall
    where the river begins.

Fruits of Winter

Running freely
  from Hoffmann's crown,
    Red Peak
      and Sentinel Dome,
  racing along the terrain
    to an off-the-rim rain
— cataracts
  from the Maker's throne —
    collected
      in the river's run;
  outrageous
    in a fickle spring
— a quiet green
    by summer's end,
  reflecting all
    that He has done.

By Campfire Light

Orange coals
    near aching soles
       help me savor you
  — Yosemite —
       for a day of light
        of fulfillment and sight;
and a prayer for you
  — Yosemite —
     that you remain this way,
    safe from complacency,
a revered and clear
    Yosemite.

Akin to the Place

Toddling
    from stay to stay,
  the '40s
    saw my inception,
  while from hatcheries
    to the bearful camps,
  the '50s were staged
    under campfire smog
     and raining coals
      from Firefalls,
with *Indian Love Call*
  an anthem.

Made a '60s run
    from Curry to Vietnam,
  with Grand Canyon
    sandwiched in.

Took some vows
  near Yosemite Falls
    to open the '70s.

Stayed in touch
  — one summer to the next —
    through a blur
      of rearing children.

Opened my eyes
  in the '90s
    to finally look around.

Yosemite Chapel
— 1879 —

That steepled brown
 house of prayer
 was assembled
 — to be —
a fount for me:
one friend,
one love,
and one destiny.

For Suzie
June 5, 1971

Yosemite Gigantea

Red pillars
    holding the sky aloft,
  age-old columns
    in my Master's house;
three groves
    of wonderment and light,
  filled with serenity
    and humbling height.

Booking a Room

Laying three dollars down
for some vacant ground
in Sunnyside —
where climbers string ropes
up four-story rocks
or between evergreens,
practicing their craft
or a high wire act,
much closer to earth
than El Cap.

Assessing Serenity

Melodic walls,
   harmonizing
      with the breeze,
   quieting
      any argument,
   stifling
      all discord.

Comforting walls
      of perspective
 — a fortress
      for repair.

Rising Light

The reliable sun
   bathes Tissiack's face
      in goldenlight,
   before the dying flame
      of an infusive day
   — ignites —
in the heights
   of a Yosemite night.

Islands of Repair

Walk along the river,
    away from your bed,
  to a place
    that's always there,
      a thought or two ahead,
    a spot
      where you can leave
        the bother far behind,
  and weigh
    what Yosemite
      has to offer.

Cathedral Heights

The red-tailed one
hovers 'round,
sketching eloquent designs
in an optimist's sky —
spurning urban sprawl
and shopping malls
for silvery spires
and three-fold grace.

While Night Hiking

How blinding,
   my flashlight,
      self-centered in my eye —
a light dissolved
   when trained
      at the full moon's might —
a moon lost
   in the blue
      of a sun's daylight —
a sun once ravenous,
   now shaded
      by the Maker's night.

Pohono's Blast

The veil swirls
    'round her base,
  while a sullen wind
    blows winter
      in your face,
yet
    the Lady stands
    — undaunted —
    regally robed
      in descending grace.

Mornings Apart

Huffing to the trailside,
   I cleared a proper path
     for a symmetrical family of four
   to snake a breakfast dash
     up the unrelenting switchbacks
       on the Yosemite Falls trail,
but set on conditioning,
   they slipped obliviously by
     the yellow striped green serpent
       who bent gracefully 'cross their track,
and the tiny lavender butterfly
   who paused to perch on my pack
     — with powder wings extended —
     the object of my walk.

Collectibles at My Feet

Round pebbles,
  and smooth
    scraps of wood
— found ebony,
    warmstone
      and amber —
    settled
      on the bleached sand;
so close
    to the river bed,
    though miles
      from Tissiack,
        towering
          overhead.

Cabin in the Grove

Clark's cabin in the trees,
— humbled —
by all the immensity,
by those pillars of worth,
with their roots
gripping the earth;
that simple product
of Clark's resign
stands sheltered
by God's design.

Near Nevada

Your immaculate garden
　　lives undaunted,
　　　where the trail
　　　　meets the stream,
　a garden
　　green-stalked
　　　and yellow topped,
　　with patient strokes
　　　of lavender in-between:
　　the blossoming
　　　offspring
　　　　of winterwhite.

Cathedral Beach

Once
 a summer's place
  to pluck four strings,
 and sing of flowers
  "gone to graveyards,
   everyone."

Now
 some space to stand
 — thoughtful —
  at river's hand
 to release
  a buoyant piece
   of ponderosa bark.

Here in the Real World

Oh radioblurt
         blaring bright,
      how obnoxious
            your digital light,
      alarming me
         to a day
            of monotony,
another day
         outside Yosemite.

Memoriesbright

Snapshot at Valley View

We pose
in a Technicolor day,
where in
black and white times
Mom and Dad
toed a similar line;
here with the Lady behind —
spouting white
from her silvery shrine;
here where the river
meanders by,
running off
to a chaotic life.

The Tunnel Tree

In a moment
of insanity,
they whittled away
at divinity,
turning
towering nobility
into a pile of vanity.

Rites of Eventide

Meadows swarming
    with careless campers
  and gawking day trippers
    under the glow
      from the Point;
dapper diners
    breaking between courses,
  adding "Hello Glacier"
  to an Ahwahnee night;
notes floating skyward
  from a squeaky soprano
    off Mother Curry's stage
— an *Indian Love Call* —
    in the light
      of a Firefall.

Yesterdaze

Salmon eggs,
   wiggly worms
      and fishing poles,
   rising fumes
      and campground smog
         from cast-iron stoves
           and burning logs,
  the scent of bacon
        and coffee grounds
      led to scrambled eggs
      and hash browns.

Dirt roads,
   hairpin curves
      and tunnel trees,
   paternal plans,
      tuna fish
        and radiator steam,
  hasty changing
      before a ride to the sand
  brought a slosh
      through the shallows
        and frying face down.

Indian Caves and Happy Isles,
      Mirror Lake and nature trails,
scrubbing behind ears,
      and a clean pair of undies,
stoked up stoves
      for jack-of-all mommies,
blackened dogs
      and potato salad
followed by Curry shows
      and Firefalls.

Kerosene lamps
      over housekeeping tables,
stalking bears,
      and campfire tales
brought an end
      to an adventurous day,
but charred marshmallows
      and other treats
         made a Yosemite
            vacation complete.

John's Song

The crackling shed
　　from silent timber
　　　alarms all,
　　but the fawn,
　　　defying
　　　　motherly
　　　　　skepticism.

Your emotional river
　　sleeps,
　　　exhausted
　　　　by spring rage
— exanimate —
　　but for the wanton
　　　green ringlets,
　　　　eccentrically kinetic.

Your foggy shroud
　　enveloping the meadow
　　　covers all,
　　but the wary head
　　　of the maternal doe,
　　and the trees —
　　　reserving their play
　　for the afternoon breeze.

A single hawk
    upholds You,
        my friend
    — effortlessly —
        atop the glacial walls
            of Your granite pantheon,
    to invoke
        this soulful day.

My ears heed
    the force
        of falling water
— immolating identities —
    lunging,
        then plunging
            toward the grinding force
                in their union.

Time
    can be heard
        passing
    in the netherworld
        outside Your door
    yet,
        in this isolated island
            of thin silence,
                You materialize
                    in twenty-
                        twenty visions.

From "The Firefall Trilogy"

Lamenting in Black and White

What gave you
   such vision, AA?
You saw things
   I can scarcely articulate.
Your shutter caught
      the essence of artistry,
   while I can
      barely spell *Yosemite*.

Finer Dining

Blackened wieners
  on curly ends
    of unbended coat hangers,
and marshmallows
  scorched in turn,
extending from the hands
  of eager children —
covered generously
  with the dirt
    of a Yosemite day.

Sprucing it up

There's new wood
    on the walking bridge;
they replaced
    that weathered railing
      where our names
      were carved,
those brown beams,
    painted over and over
    — coating —
      but never erasing.

But now,
    there's new wood
      on the walking bridge
— a clean slate
    for the next
      generation.

Hangin' at Cathedral

By the cool Merced,
    where in beach party days,
      Michael rowed his boat
        past the sands of El Capitan
          to Sentinel up ahead;
    now where a smooth stone
      is more prized to skip
        than a one hand
          flattened beer can.

Gaining Perspective

The Valley
    of my youth
      — Firefalls,
        rising trout,
          and bears
            on the prowl —
has become
    a refuge by now:
      temple walls,
        waterfalls,
          and space
            to rejuvenate.

Summer Rain

The purifying drops
    rat-tat on canvas
        and cleanse the air
          of dusty traces
— like the water trucks
      of yesterday —
as headlong falls
    spring white
       from royal places,
    showering down
       through lesser crevices,
and the river
    runs high
      with debris,
while a smoky fog
    lingers
      in the trees.

Bears

A ferocious lot —
 breaking into cars
  like they owned the park.

Lashing out
   at ignorant folk,
 whose only crime
  is leaving
   their doggy bag behind.

There ought to be a law
  against these scruffy rogues,
   who can't keep their claws
    off the customers' leftovers.

Boulders on the Brain

Blind to the Maker's hand,
 I spent my youth
  in frivolous pursuits;
oblivious to the sculptured walls,
 I saw beach parties and Firefalls
  as the reason for it all,
 unaware that I was living in
  the remedy for most everything.

Yosemite Lament

So much for Camp 7,
"Lower River,"
or whatever you call the place
— a walking bridge away from 16,
or I guess it's called
"Housekeeping"
these days.

Gone is the scent
of coffee, bacon and burning logs
— dawning daily —
under a bright layer of campfire smog.

No more will black bears
make nightly rounds
of convenient cans
— piled high —
with table scraps and coffee grounds.

Such rich tradition,
washed down the drain,
when the river rose
above the picnic tables.

Where decision makers,
having the upper hand,
let unruly nature
have her way with the land.

So "Farewell!" to Camp 7
and carefree vacations
— gone the way of Firefalls
and service stations.

Wildlight

Mule Deer Appears

Once hidden
    in the autumn leaves,
the wide-eyed lady
    of the meadow
  — freezes —
    in a heart-racing
      pose of hesitancy,
craning
    the brain
      of her stately frame
        toward my indignity,
before stepping away
    to blend
      into the shades
        of an earthtone day.

Patience

Sporting
    a breathless stare,
  the bobcat
    stands softly
      on the fresh fallen snow,
  waiting
    for the white
      to show a twitch
        of furry life.

Two Sides of Plight

June bugs
　　crashing in
　　　indiscriminately;
　　mosquitoes, flies
　　　and the like:
　　pesky critters
　　　in a man-infested world
　　— partners —
　　　in the wild.

The American Lion

Puma,
  cougar,
    or whoever
      you are,
still lord
  of a wilderness
    being gobbled up;
  pounced on,
    and devoured
      with avaricious jaws.

High Country Eyes

The bighorn
    looks on
        in craggy sanctity,
once trifled
    in frivolous years
        of insanity,
now revived,
    with a foothold
        in recovery.

Black Bear's Despair

Garbage can banging
    and lumbering drool,
creatures of habit,
    fed by fools.

Boulder-size bruins
    in waning wilderness,
methodically slaughtered
    for acting like us.

A Coyote Afternoon

Resting
  in the hollow
    of the rock,
  the merry prankster
    pairs
      his curious side
        with the shifting wind,
  to sniff out
    a wild binge
      of winged
        and crawling things,
  or whatever's edible,
    when facing
      a winter
        of scrimping.

Yosemite Winterwatcher

The great gray
  feathers down,
    to "whoo"
      on the uprooted knuckles
        of the Jeffrey pine,
      set against
        the white remnants
          of a furious night.

Mallards

The mottled brown
    and the green-headed sheen
wing in
    to splash down
      by Cathedral Beach,
where a gathering of souls
    share an acrylic spring,
and the verdant shades
    in the river's range.

High Sierra Granite

Winter's master hand
stroked rich
the warm beige
across the silver
stone canvas,
where spring
could swirl
her chartreuse
shades of life,
caught timeless,
in the white
of midday
Yosemitelight.

Raptor's Flight

The red-tailed hawk
  and the golden eagle
prowl the peaceful skies
  above the granite Cathedral,
that the rocks and the spires
    might continue to inspire
  those petty dreamers and fools
  who we dare not lose.

Lower River Raccoon

He comes when the embers
    are losing their light,
that black-masked invader
    from out of the night.

With his furry gray body
    and beady dark eyes,
he's here for the garbage
    or the trout on ice.

A fisherman unrivaled,
    he savors his catch,
but given the time,
    he'd sooner have mine.

Then his ring tail will trail
    his rotund rear end,
as he waddles away
    to some other buffet.

Swallowtail Doubletake

A black stri-ped
  yellow surprise,
    caught wingingly wide,
  amid a kaleidoscope
    of blooming
      meadowlight.

Squirrel's Play

From my rest stop on the rim,
    to the campground down below,
  the voracious gray
    goes scrambling from his hole.

With a billowing tail
    tacked to an ample behind,
  he pauses over haunches
    with swinish thoughts in mind.

Then he twitches a whisker
    at my stingy disposition,
  before adjusting his design
    to a more devious proposition.

Steller's Jay's Foray

Raucous sleep robber
    and breakfast beggar —
the indigo blue
    sounds his gluttonous cry
      from the limbs
        of the incense cedar,
then glides
    down the splinters
      of morning glitter,
to hop, hop over
    and beak crusts of bread.

Trailsides

Yosemite Hiking

We move out,
    eager to seek
those things
    that together
    we find
will harmonize
    our incongruous
minds.

Yosemite Ascent

The prized summits
> on this crowded sphere
are reserved
for those
> who earn them.

Illusive Lakelight

Dawn's alpine plane
   ruffled
     by the afternoon;
   the inborn
     gift of morning
      — muddled —
     by an ascending sun,
   not to mend
     'til evening comes.

South Rim Promenade

Follow the trail
    of the wind,
      west from Glacier Point,
     to where
    you can savor
     the wild air
      along the view.

Wade
    through the green seas
    laced with yellow
      white
      and violet
to where the bloody-red
   snow flowers
     hide among the trees.

Trailside Repose

The kind glacier
    polished the hollow
in the erratic
    it left behind,
a place
    where I can settle
and leech fatigue
    from my weary mind,
by watching the water
    as it tumbles by,
rushing off
    to make white traces
        along wonder-wide eyes.

High Country Drizzle

With the first drops
    from a starless ceiling,
a poncho
    becomes a shelter of sorts
— humble accommodations —
    though solitary
    and secure.

The Four Mile Trail

One foot after the other,
  the other after the first,
    trudging up the switchbacks
    on the Four Mile Trail.

Yosemite on my left,
  Yosemite on my right,
    following Muir's whiskers
    up the Four Mile Trail.

Laptops to the left,
  cellphones to the right
    — it's Glacier Point
    in cyberlight!

Two chews of jerky
  and a handful of grapes,
    back into the solace
    of the Four Mile Trail.

Bewilderness

Weighing the merits
    of turning around,
  against a dozen more switchbacks
    and a four hundred foot climb.

Enter the ouzel,
    the undaunted one,
  swimming up rapids
    — more fish than fowl.

At the top of the rise,
    above the uncertainty,
  larkspur and lilies
    — reward for tenacity.

Snow Creek Retreat

A hidden treat
   up the veiled path
      along Tenaya Creek,
  above the mirror
     that's turning to sand,
  to where you find yourself
      — reflecting —
    beside contentment's pond.

Vantage Points

Tracking down serenity,
   step by step,
  from high atop Half Dome
   to a meadow down below,
  looking for an island
   — a place to breathe —
  where you can weigh bother
   against an afternoon breeze.

Off Again

Into the wilderness
— exhilaration lead on —
up John Muir's Trail
to the source of it all,
packing visions
of waterfalls,
sunsets,
and such,
eager to trade
complacency
for a red-tailed hawk.

Assessing the Climb

Worth the price
— those shooting stars
above the switchbacks
— that eyeful of Nevada
from the John Muir Trail;
expectation
— exceeded —
around every bend;
the burning pain
— a bargain —
up against the gain.

In Sight of Nevada

Splashed yellow
    and stalky green,
  the steely walls
      rear arnica
        all rooted in cracks,
      clutching the sustenance
        of winters past
        — alive —
        in the vitality
          of spring.

Above Nevada

An aching back
>from a weighty pack
fits the grind
of a staircase climb;
self-distrust
and weariness
adjudged the price
for hiking higher.

Little Yosemite Afternoon

Passing some time
in a sugar pine
— waiting out the drops —
a bank above
the river's run,
where a hollow serves
as a "scribble den."

A Little Yosemite Repose

Come Douglas squirrel
    and Steller's jay,
  come view what's left of me,
    sprawled comeuppant
      along my bag,
        head resting on my pack.

Ten miles of trail
    on a well-abused frame
— feeling every step,
    though relishing the pain;
inhaling
    what remains of the day,
    picturing the splendor
    I passed along the way.

Moraine Dome Night

As the last of a drizzle
　　— sizzles out —
　　　in the remains of a fire,
　the fleeing clouds
　　— reveal —
　a festival of light
　　rivaling the river's roar
　　　for uppermost in mind.

Waiting on the Weather

Under the granite overhang,
biding time
with a splash
of scarlet penstemon,
knees pulled
out of the rain,
hearing an ouzel
enliven the bony pine
with song sweet
as fatigue in retrospect —
there where the river
flows green to the bridge,
before dancing white
down the ravine.

A Merced Lake Oration

The elder statesman
— with his frenetic gray hair
    wildly tousled about —
piddling around the camp,
    chewing both sides
        of the fat,
had me wondering
    if I'm destined
        for such a chat,
    and whether Muir
        — in all his sauntering —
            took more than one part.

A Merced Lake Afternoon

Holding the granite,
   a bluff above
     the high Sierra camp,
watching
   the river's howling tumble
     into a placid stretch,
wondering
   what took me so long,
to rise above complacency
and let wilderness
   have her way.

Topping Hoffmann

Scrambling up
  Muir's mountain
    to stick your head
      into the blue,
up above the domes
    and earthly stuff
— up where
  the air is elixir —
where a scan'll
  get you Cathedral Peak,
    Mt. Clark,
      and Tissiack,
with the Grand Canyon
  of the Tuolumne
      running 'cross your back.

Light in a May Lake Night

A blaze across the way
    above the opposite shore,
  a reflection of which
    stretches along the blackened glass
— a warm orange line
    from that campfire to mine,
      and hopefully back again.

Just Hours Away from the Everyday

Savoring
  the starlit darkness
    of a moonless May Lake night,
  as a campfire
    on the far shore
      sends out
        its orange stripe;
wishing
  there were more days
    in a Yosemite week
    —less need for sleep—
while recalling
  the scarlet penstemon
    that rivaled the view
      near Hoffman's peak.

Savoring Pohono

Poking along the rim,
from Glacier Point
to a parking lot —
stopping at Sentinel Fall,
Taft Point
and behind Cathedral Rocks;
though a versicolored garden
laced with iridescent wings
is the wonder of wonders
on the trail of the wind.

Yosemite on My Mind

I live
  to clear
    city soot
      from my lungs,
        so I might breathe
          serenity,
  to climb
  — misted —
      through a second wind,
        and know one certainty:
    that if heaven
      were to be
        Yosemite,
  you'd hear
    no complaints
      from me.

Yosemite's Final Say

Near
the weathered pine,
a warming blaze
takes the chill away
— rising
in day's final phase —
to chide
the shivering night,
for falling
along the lines
of otherwise.

Panorama Calling

Oh come with me now
 from the point on the peak
  down to Illilouette Creek
   where the snow flower grows,
  up the switchbacks of pain
— soothed by Yosemite sublimity —
to the plateau of light,
 where the Valley
  bursts into sight,
down the rambling slope,
 to where Nevada
  roars white
   into enlivened eyes.

The Mist Trail

Up, up
    the granite staircase,
  to where
    the widest of white
      showers
        her thundering light
    through my shivering
      flood of fulfillment.

A Respite on JM's Trail

From every black crack
    in the dank wall,
the bright yellow
    messengers
      of light
    — spring —
atop
    lively green pedestals,
invigorated
      by melting winterwhite.

In the Shadow of Nevada

Your blossoms,
   all coral and golden
     above their green,
    thriving against
     the pitchy bed
      of the stream.

Nevada Falling

Before safe railings,
    the watery greens and blues
      turn a deafening white,
crashing violently
    toward a lower path;
as says my cautious side,
    "Some of Nature's treasures
      are best left at a distance."

Pohono Passage

Roam
    below Sentinel Dome,
along the path
    of the summer breeze,
to where the wildflowers
        are scattered about
    like litter
        on a city street.

Atop Nevada

Grateful hikers
　　break on smooth stone,
　　　as children
　　　　wade in waiting water,
before the river
　　whitens down,
　　　along the eyes
　　　　above distant smiles.

Island in the Sky

The meadows green
    and top-lighted stone
all silvery clean
    and Godly to the bone.
    Tuolumne
— that beckoning sound —
the air of the spring,
    issued by the wind,
        so far from routine.

Nearing the Point

A glimmering light
        graced my trail today,
    "Taking it slow,
        taking it slow."

A patient partner
    begged his pardon,
        as he crumpled to rest,
        "He never gets tired of seeing
            this, though."

So I lowered my pack
        to sit by his side,
    seeing
        there was much to know.

Looking Over the Shoulder

Give me the strength
　　to climb the shoulder,
　there to ponder
　a final ascent,
up that crude
　　granite footpath,
　　　one weary step
　　　　above a second thought,
　where I might plod
　on up the cables
　　to the treasures
　　at the top.

Topping Tissiack

Clutching the cable
  in a sole-scraping shuffle
  up the granite,
  from board to board
  to the top —
from self doubt
  to adulation
  at the top,
prized in arriving
  above the view.

Ascending Half Dome

Hauling your weight
   up the cables
      to Tissiack's crown —
hand after burning hand,
      perch after precarious perch.

Muir said,
  work hard for beauty,
  here,
    as anywhere on earth.

Among the Giants

Wandering
　　through the sequoias
— perusing the *Good Book* —
　savoring
　　those words
　　　that were literally
　　　　beat into Muir,
　praying
　　he could appreciate
　　　each phrase;
with every bless-ed verse
　being rooted
　　in the Author
　　　of these trees.

Pausing Briefly

Up from the camp,
　　along Bridalveil Creek,
　there's a pocket
　　of peace
　　　by the path
　　　　to the lake,
　a place
　　where the alpine green
　　　attends the chatter
　　　　of the stream —
　　and mosquitoes
　　　grow bigger
　　　　than birds.

In Memory of Evans and Lowell,
who walked with me there.

A Way of Passage

Trailing
  the mysteries
    of Tenaya Canyon
  —sandwiched between—
    Basket and Half Dome,
following
  that precarious path
  along the creek,
saddened
  that Ahwaneechees
    would see it
      as a means of flight,
fleeing the demons
  who'd spirit them
    from paradise.

Wawonasuite

Wandering on the Wawona Green

Wawona Welcome

The lamp
   atop the square granite post
glares
   above dead vines,
     which I believe
       were once flourishing hops.

Its mate
  shines brightly
   over billowing green foliage,
that covers
  what I assume
    is a square granite post.

Wawona Afternoon

As the sun-bonneted woman
    bent forward,
  to address
    the crimson
      croquet ball,
    she ultimately tested
      that broad swath of material
        covering her backside.

Wawona Landscape

The yellow snapdragon
   climbs predictably
      above the weathered brass sundial,
   casting its shadow
      on the tarnished face
      of the pedestalled timepiece
         that sits splitting
            a triangular flower bed
   — found flourishing —
         in warm reds and low pastels
            on the bright white
               hotel side of the square.

Wawona Reception

"I see T-R-O-U-B-L-E!"
blared in stereo
from the rented ballroom
atop the pro shop,
as the black and white wedding
was now sandwiched
below a layer
of long-reserved rooms.

Fresh from the green
of lawn promises,
the party left a litter
of tables and chairs.

A Wawona Home

Green shuttered and gabled,
   the white two-story haven
     snuggles up cozy against the hill,
  warm puffs rising
    from a welcome stone chimney,
      to cover the scent of evergreen.

Wawona Farewell

The frosty white letters
    on the forest green sign,
   hitched to the white picket gate
     that separates the neatly cropped lawn
      from the empty pool,
  reads:
   "Hotel Guests Only!"

Lymanlight

Yosemite Valleylight

There's no darkness
    down below,
  just trees and snow
    below alpenglow.

The picture
    of a wholesome time,
  before fast food,
    swimming pools
      and traffic jams.

The moon peers down
    as in Lyman's mind,
  but the Muirish glow
    has tarnished with time.

Yosemite Alpenglow

Heir to the Place

The bear was there
    when Mom and Dad were young,
but long gone
    by the time I was born.

Still a symbol
    of a state
    — that's lost
    the spirit
      of the land —
    the grizzly
      lopes on
        by Lyman's hand.

Uzumati — The Great Bear of Yosemite

Yosemite Campfirelight

A pyramid
    of molten might,
  you fork your tongues
    at the wild night.

Warm shades of amber
    fuel your desire,
  sending wood-born incense
    to a high-Sierra sky.

The melting heat
    of marshmallow days,
  a minstrel's blaze,
    this poet's pyre.

The centerpiece
    for a circle of smiles —
  tend it well
    you guardians of the fire.

A Mountain Campfire

A Parting Ray of Daylight

Such is the plan
    of the Master hand,
  to part the gossamer
      at the first sign of night,
letting the last flash
    of a winter's sun
    paint silver-faced Tissiack
    a goldenlight.

Dance of Cloud and Cliff

Cathedralight

Dual spires
    rising to radiant skies,
  mark the temple
   that's captured
    in Lyman's sight.

— *Cathedral* —

It's a place
   in Yosemite,
    where God shaped the granite
    to say, "It's Me."

Cathedral Snow

Weary Campfirelight

Once ablaze
    against a risky night,
  you grew to enrich
    an impromptu site,
  by raising your flames
    before tiring eyes,
  then spending your coals
    to warm shivering souls.

Now surrender
    to the dawning light,
  yet hold a spark
    deep in your heart,
  that might turn kindling
    into a rising fire.

Embers at Dawn

First Light

Muir said,
    "it changes you forever."

I say,
    it washes the city away,
        and takes the doldrums
           from your day.

Tunnel View,
    Valley View,
any view
    that brings her
        into sight

— *Yosemite* —

freeing her colors
    to define light.

Evening Glow in Yosemite

Winter's Firelight

Clear away enough white
    from the cold winter ground
  to set fire
    to a tinder pile
  of branches and twigs
    and a Yule log or two,
whatever providence provides;
  that we might weather the night,
  a bittersweet night,
were it not
  for the sweet warming light.

Fire Dance

Breath Stop at the Top

At the end
of the granitelight,
where the silver
gives way to the sky,
near where Yosemite Creek
turns a regal white,
before the Emperor
drops out of sight
— there's a rooftop seat —
where a soul
can be left alone
with everything
from Mt. Clark
to Sentinel Dome.

That stop,
near trail's end,
where the skyline's
a most welcome friend.

Yosemite Landscape

Clark's Mountain

Your citadel joins the heavens
    in an air of alpenglow,
  like your silver-laden giant
    in the Mariposa Grove.

Springing from the heart
    of Muir's "range of light,"
  you mount a golden challenge
    to the invading night.

Colors of Twilight

A Lantern's Life

Beat-up and rusted,
    a relic of crude design,
        reeking of kerosene —
      a hand-me-down
          from a simpler time.

That creaky lamp
    hangs still
      among the icicles,
    to brighten
      a sheltered porch
and define
      a welcome door.

It's well-tended glass
    lets out
      the goldenlight,
    to draw home a child,
      or receive
        a wayward stranger
        in the night.

Lantern Light

Fading Light

"Pywiack,"
   the Ahwahneechee lake
    of shining rocks;
that land
   where Tenaya
    made his last stand;
those waters
   — slowly filling with sand —
will soon join the Miwoks,
   driven from their land.

Lake of the Shining Rocks

Moonfirelight

Not all is darkness
in the night,
not with the lights
of the night;
certainly not
with moonfirelight
— that mingling
of lunar bright
and campfire light;
and the reflection
of each,
on the lake
at the head of my bed.

Moonfire

Riverlight

In warm shadows,
   I follow you
    — my Merced —
   as you snake away
     from this vagabond day,
   to a place
    where blue heron
     and native trout play;
a place
   that's bright
    around the bend,
   where stone green water's
    a reliable friend.

Riparian Riches

Pinnacle Light

Lyman's brush
    caught Half Dome's side,
and the face that glows
    in alpenlight;
that pose
    that Olmsted's view affords,
that peak that looms
    in the hiker's mind;
away from any thought
    of an up-the-cables romp,
more to savor the sweat
    of a patient climb;
to conquer your fears
    and inadequacies,
there to linger
    at the Maker's feet.

The Light of Tissiack

In Vernal Light

The Big White
    paints her loud stripe
  down the silvery granite wall,
as I climb
— refreshed —
  up the watery steps
    of perpetual rain.

What price?
  Soggy fatigue.
What prize?
  That rainbow down below.

Dance of Water and Light

Falcon's Flight

Almost hidden
    by the darkness
      in the light,
    the Peregrine shines
      in golden Tissiack's sight.

Nearly depleted
    by the hand of man,
    the raptor
      still has a place
        in God's perfect plan.

Perched precariously
    on the Valley wall,
    that hand of man
      may yet
        cause the Falcon to fall.

Return of the Falcon

Light from the Other Side

Ahwahnee
— the deep grassy Valley —
that taste of eternity.

All your light
and life —
your everything in sight.

A place
to extol
and rinse the bother
from your soul.

To stand
— renewed —
with divinity
in view.

Ahwahnee — The Deep Grassy Valley

A Light in a Dreamer's Night

There's a campfire
　　high atop
　　　the temple wall,
　thriving there
　as a beacon
　　in the night
　　　— by the point
　　　of the Arrow —
　　　　a welcome light;
　catching the eye
　　of a flat-faced King —
　　　half-haloed in gossamer
　　　　and dusted with white.

There's a campfire
　　high atop
　　　the temple wall,
　overlooking the site
　　of God's perfect delight.

Warmed by the View

A Light Still Shining

He made me
    see wilderness
        through his eyes,
that after
    a lifetime
        of Yosemites,
I might see
    what was there
        all along.

On Stephen Lyman's Birthday

From Indian Canyon
    to Eagle Peak,
      breathing the North Rim
        on Stephen Lyman's birthday;
from fatigue to consecration,
      tracing his fanciful steps,
    along a Yosemite landscape
      to a seat above alpenglow;
recalling the windows he opened
      to a place I thought I knew,
    sampling his understanding,
      and warmed by the view.

August 16, 1999

Christmaslight

Ahwahnee Christmas

El Capitan
  and Cathedral Rocks
    dusted white
— enlivened —
  with gossamer
    and descending light.

Incense cedar
  and ponderosa pine,
    standing breathless
      at Bridalveil's side.

All God's creation,
  reverently waiting
    for the birthday
      of the King.

Christmas 1998 — Valley View

Chapel Light

The porch light burns
above the chapel door
— a beacon —
to a weary traveler
— a salvation —
in the storm.

The light shines bright
on a Yosemite morn;
a lamp of warmth
and Christmas cheer;
a blaze of promise
in the winter of your year.

Christmas 1999 — Yosemite Chapel

Pohono Glow

The light of Christmas
is on Bridalveil and Leaning Tower,
a fixture in a fleeting world,
a ray of faith
in the face of uncertainty,
illuminating the dreary stratus
in your winter of despair —
a flicker of the Maker
in this solemn season,
and a harbinger of hope
for the coming year.

Christmas 2000 — Bridalveil Fall

Cathedral Sunrise

The saintly mist of Christmas
endows the steely walls
with angel's lace
and promises of smiles
— enthralling our squinting eyes —
as Yosemite glow
enlivens the snow
on the Maker's morn.

Christmas 2001 — Cathedral Spires

Yosemite Alacrity

Set for the season,
the Emperor
drapes his misty cape
along the wintry wall.
Robed in light,
the regal one
— lets fall —
a sacred Christmas cheer,
and a stately prayer
for a bless-ed new year.

Christmas 2002 — Yosemite Falls

Yosemite Shining

Shapely evergreens,
dusted white,
and spiny seasonals
caked with light,
behold Bridalveil's
stately flight,
at this hopeful
Christmas time —
a time of promise
and a time of prayer,
for a reign of kindness
and a peace-FULL new year.

Christmas 2003 — Bridalveil Fall

Christmas in the Grove

Giant sequoias,
who witnessed
the first Christmas,
have risen
to herald
this latest edition
— chosen —
from all God's creation
to hallow them all.

Sequoia 2004 — Grant Grove

Ahwahnee Calling

The Valley sends greetings
> for a meaningful season:
Yosemite
> — alive —
> in holiday greens
>> and winter whites,
> silver granite walls
— a temple of light —
> heralding a peaceful period
>> of heightened spirituality
and a prayer
> for a prosperous new year.

Yosemite 2005 — Tunnel View

Holiday Walk

Take a stroll across Sentinel Meadow,
shedding your bother along the way
— letting Yosemite have its say.
Leach the bitterness
from a troublesome winter,
and a soothing breeze
from reliable Ahwahnee
will loosen your leaves of care,
and ferry them from this sacred season
of hope and rejuvenation.

Yosemite 2006 — Yosemite Falls from Sentinel Meadow

About The Author

Warren Cederborg is a graduate of California State University at Hayward in theatre arts and speech with extensive postgraduate work in English literature. A longtime journalist, freelance writer and educator, *The Mysemite Sketches* is his fourth published work. Early in 2004, Cederborg's debut novel *Sacred Ground* was released by AuthorHouse, followed two years later by *Where the Osprey Flies*, his fictional account of conflicting relationships set in the Northwest. Thirty years earlier, as a professional bridge player, he complied a technical book on the game. An award winning photographer (a sample of his work can be seen on the front cover), Cederborg is a Vietnam veteran who has two grown children and resides in Visalia, California with his wife Suzie.

Printed in the United States
71651LV00005B/55-162